# People in the Community

# Dentists

## Diyan Leake

**Heinemann** LIBRARY

## www.heinemann.co.uk/library
Visit our website to find out more information about Heinemann Library books.

To order:
- ☎ Phone 44 (0) 1865 888066
- 🖹 Send a fax to 44 (0) 1865 314091
- 💻 Visit the Heinemann Bookshop at www.heinemann.co.uk/library to browse our catalogue and order online.

First published in Great Britain by Heinemann Library, Halley Court, Jordan Hill, Oxford OX2 8EJ, part of Pearson Education. Heinemann is a registered trademark of Pearson Education Ltd.

Editorial: Diyan Leake and Catherine Clarke
Design: Joanna Hinton-Malivoire and Steve Mead
Picture research: Tracy Cummins and Heather Mauldin
Production: Alison Parsons

Origination: Chroma Graphics (Overseas) Pte Ltd
Printed and bound in China by South China Printing Company Ltd

ISBN  978 0 431 19242 0
12 11 10 09 08
10 9 8 7 6 5 4 3 2 1

**British Library Cataloguing in Publication Data**
Leake, Diyan
Dentists. - (People in the community)
617.6
A full catalogue record for this book is available from the British Library.

**Acknowledgments**
The publishers would like to thank the following for permission to reproduce photographs:
©Age Fotostock pp. **4** (Werner Otto), **9** (Sylvain Grandadam) **22 (top)** (Werner Otto); ©Alamy (Peter Griffin) p. **5**; ©Corbis pp. **7** (FotostudioFM/Zefa), **11** (Peter Beck), **16** (Lucidio Studio, Inc.), **17** (Tom Stewart), **20** (Simon Marcus), **22** (Peter Beck); ©Getty Images pp. **8** (Jon Riley), **10** (PNC), **12** (Paul Burns), **13** (Paul Burns), **18** (Wayne Eastep), **19** (Karin Dreyer), **21** (Chabruken); ©Heinemann-Raintree (Tracy Cummins) pp. **14**, **22 (middle)**; ©Jupiter Images (Anderson Ross) p. **6**; ©Robert & Linda Mitchell p. **15**.

Front cover photograph of a dentist reproduced with permission of ©Getty Images. Back cover photograph reproduced with permission of ©Getty Images (Karin Dreyer).

Every effort has been made to contact copyright holders of any material reproduced in this book. Any omissions will be rectified in subsequent printings if notice is given to the publisher.

# Contents

# Communities

People live in communities. They live near each other and help each other.

People work together in a
community.

# Dentists in the community

Dentists work in communities.

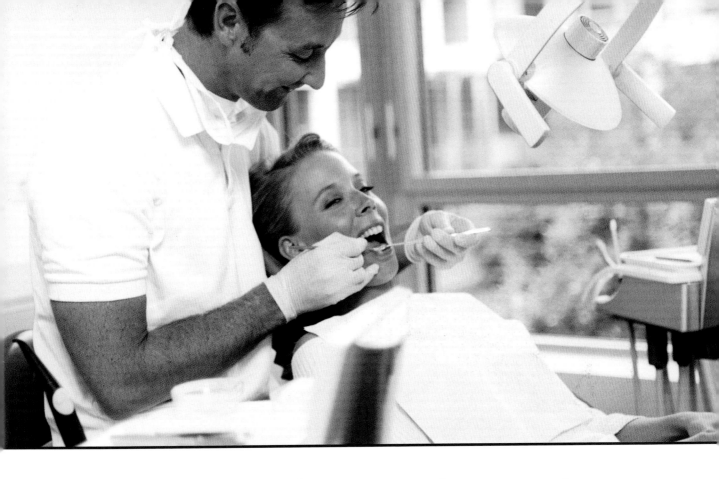

Dentists look after people's teeth.

# What dentists do

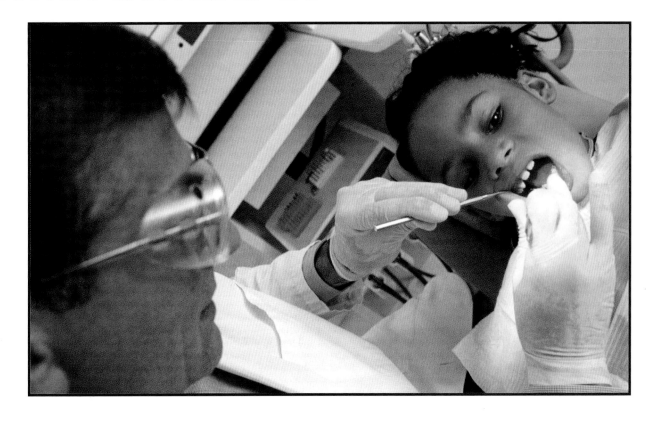

Dentists check teeth to make sure
they are not going bad.

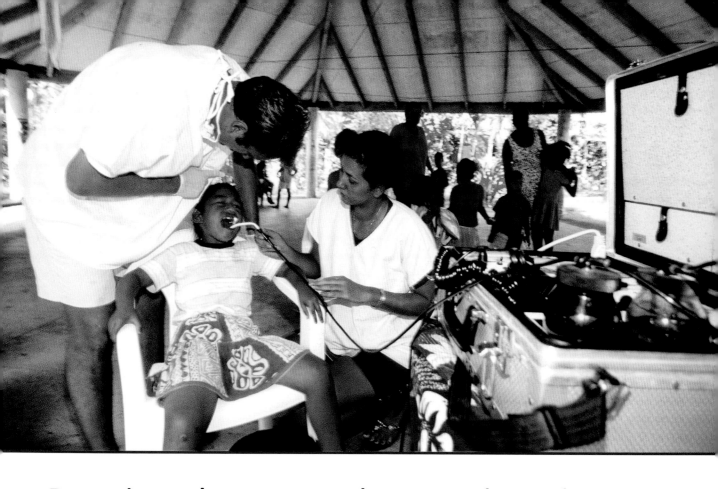

Dentists clean people's teeth with a special tool.

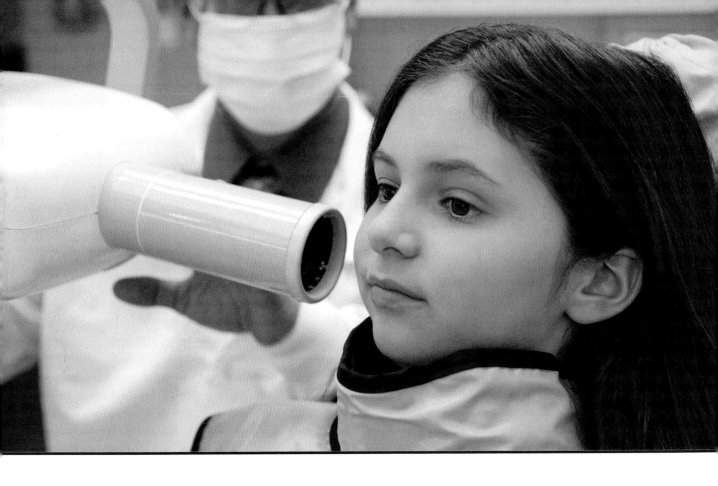

Dentists take X-rays of teeth to make sure they are not going bad.

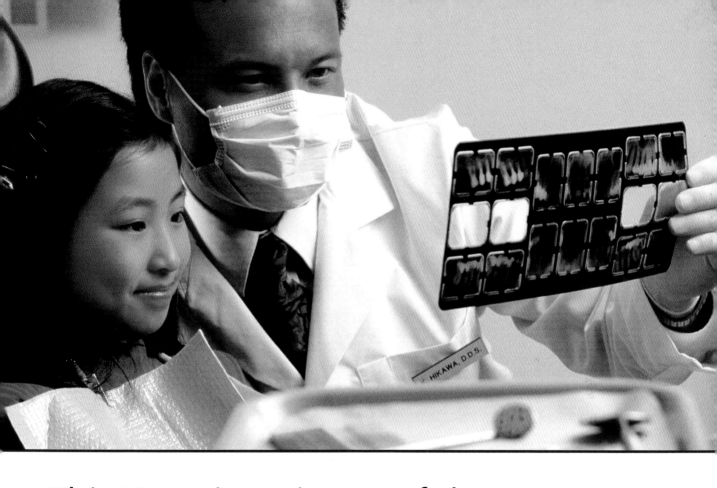

This X-ray is a picture of the girl's teeth.

# What dentists use

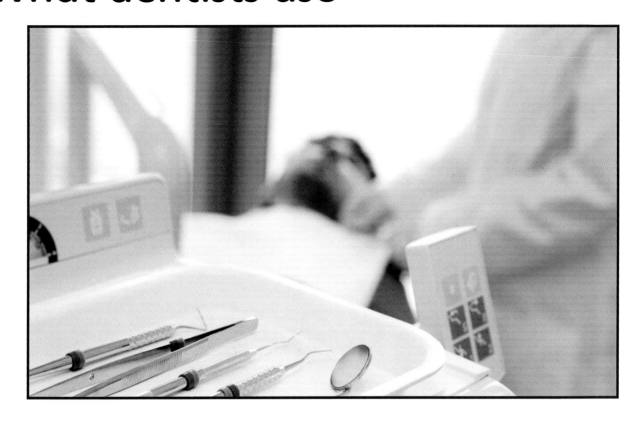

Dentists use lots of different tools.

mirror

Dentists use mirrors to look at teeth.

# Where dentists work

Dentists work in offices.

Dentists work in clinics.

# People who work with dentists

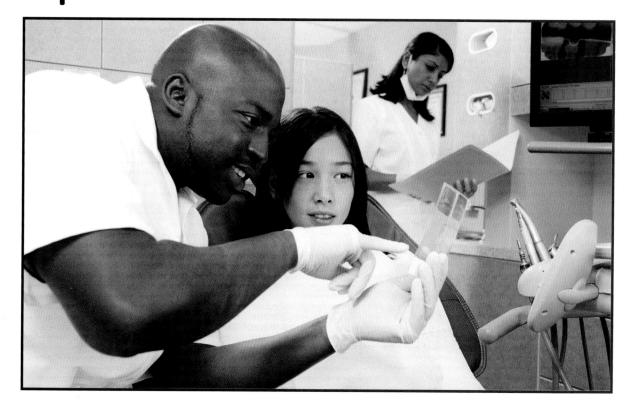

Dentists work with other people.

This person greets people.

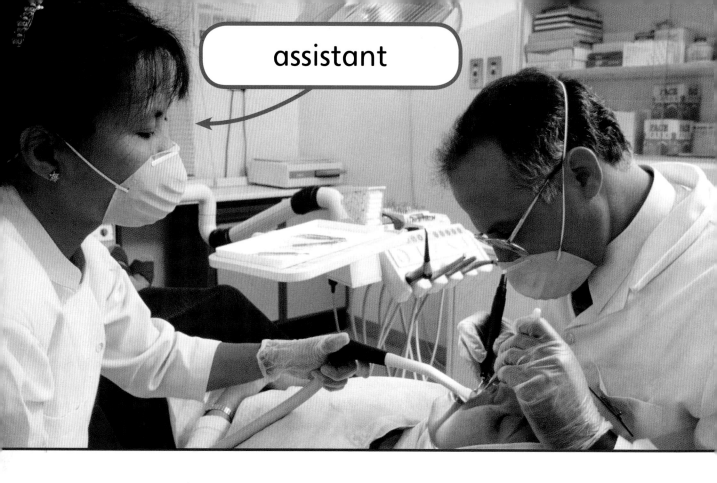

This person helps the dentist. She gives the dentist the right tools.

hygienist

This person helps to clean teeth so they do not go bad.

# How dentists help us

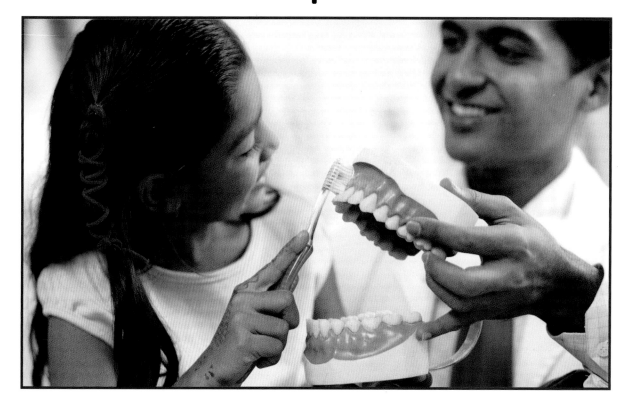

Dentists help keep our teeth healthy.
They show us how to brush our teeth.

Dentists help the community.

# Picture glossary

 **community**  group of people living and working in the same area

 **office**  place where a dentist works

 **X-ray**  photo of the inside of a person's body

# Index

# Notes for parents and teachers

This series introduces readers to the lives of different community workers, and explains some of the different jobs they perform around the world. Some of the locations featured include Hanover, Germany (page 4); Ua Pou, French Polynesia (page 9); Chicago, USA (page 14), and Siem Reap, Cambodia (page 15).

**Before reading**
Talk to the children about the work of a dentist. Ask if they have been to the dentist. Have they ever had toothache? What did it feel like? Why do they think people get toothache? What different people did they see at the dentist's?

**After reading**
• Help the children to draw large smiley faces with teeth. Put these on the wall as a collage.
• To the tune of "Here we go round the mulberry bush" sing the following and encourage the children to make the actions:
*This is the way we brush our teeth...*
*This is the way we rinse our mouth...*
*This is the way we smile at our friends...*